SWAY

THE INSIDE SECRETS THE TOP 1% USE TO INFLUENCE POLICY CHANGE AND GET WHAT THEY WANT AND HOW YOU CAN TOO

JOHN THIBAULT

HOW TO CHANGE A LAW

"You can make a difference in your community. With this book you can actually create laws in your city, county or state."

ROBERT A. SCHULLER NEW YORK TIMES
BEST-SELLING AUTHOR, WALKING IN
YOUR OWN SHOES

"How to Change a Law" provides step-by-step, insider knowledge about how to enact or amend a statute."

STEVE CHURCHWELL, CHURCHWELL
WHITE LLP, AND FORMER GENERAL
COUNSEL, CALIFORNIA FAIR POLITICAL
PRACTICES COMMISSION

For permission requests, write to
"Permissions Coordinator"
iLobby LLC
325 Sharon Park Drive, #210
Menlo Park, CA 94025

Published in the United States of America

Publisher iLobby

For more information on 90-Minute Books including finding out how you can publish your own book, visit 90minutebooks.com or call (863) 318-0464

 Formatted with Vellum

DISCLAIMER

This book is for educational purposes only and does not constitute an alternative to legal or other professional advice. The publisher and author make no representations or warranties with respect to the accuracy or completeness of the contents of this book and disclaim any liability to any party with respect to any loss, damage, or disruption caused, or alleged to have been caused, by errors, omissions, information, or programs contained herein. Any resemblance to actual persons, either living or dead, businesses, companies, events, or locales is coincidental. References are provided for informational purposes only and do not constitute endorsement of any websites or other sources.

CONTENTS

INTRODUCTION

I think you'd agree with me that voters around the country are generally pretty frustrated, whether they're on the left or the right. They have been doing things that have been ineffective in terms of making change. If you look at modeling—who is succeeding—there are small pockets or groups of people who are doing it the right way and generally have higher levels of success. They are often part of big corporations that have strong government affairs offices, big unions, or trade associations—the top 1%.

I want to empower voters to start thinking about ways they can engage in civil discourse in public policy to change lives and have better lives themselves.

Being able to share this message is important to me so I asked professional interviewer Susan Austin to help capture my thoughts and bring them together in this book. What follows is a conversation you can join in with as I share my thoughts on the inside secrets the top 1% use to influence policy change, get what they want and how you can too.

I hope this book educates you on the importance of having your voice heard, but also learning to take action in a civil way. Hopefully, this inspires you to engage in a real way, so you can get something done.

To Your Bigger Voice!

John Thibault

ONE

WHY IS IT SO HARD TO INFLUENCE POLICY CHANGE?

SUSAN: I'm excited to have the opportunity to talk with you John, and help share your thoughts and ideas on how the top 1% use influence and policy changes to get what they want.

Let's start by addressing why it's so hard to influence policy changes in today's world?

JOHN: Policymaking and politics have become so complex that individual voters don't know how to access Washington, the state capitals, or even sometimes local city councils.

In the past, this would have been easier because a smaller number of people were engaged. Now there are a lot more issues and complicated technology. Over the past 20-30 years it has become increasingly difficult to be heard above the noise and actually make a difference. Two key elements have contributed to this and the effects can be seen in today's political climate.

First, when people are content, they don't engage in politics. When the economy is good, they generally aren't very involved, although there is always a small core of people who will be. Then as we end up with difficult decisions to make or polarization as we see now in Congress and even in some states, people want to have their voices heard, and they would like their votes to matter, but it becomes more challenging for them to get something done.

The second challenge is the number of individual constituents in a district. 150 years ago, the population was much smaller and the number of constituents was somewhere between 30,000 and 50,000 per representative in Congress. After 1900, the government decided to lock the number of representatives at 435 (I'm primarily referring to the House of Representatives) but the population didn't stop growing when that happened. In 1900, the population was 76 million, it was 282 million in 2000, and now it's over 315 million. Today that means for every representative, you are 1 of 700,000 people in your district—unlike 200 years ago, when you would have been 1 of 50,000.

As the population grows and the ratio adjusts, it's going to become increasingly difficult to meet with your representative to be heard and get something done because there are more of us and the same number of them. The ratio is working against us.

Voters need to realize the old methods may not work the way they thought. What you probably hear a lot is if you want to get something done, call your congressman or write them a letter; call talk radio, write an editorial in your local newspaper, etc. In the old "analog" world, those would have been good things to do. The only difference is you're doing it on a one-off basis.

You are ONE of 700,000 people. You're trying to make

a difference, but what you don't realize is there are professionals who are working this every single day. If you don't decide what you want to get done, there are other people who will decide for you. Now there are small, special-interest groups of people who decide how things happen, and the general public is not involved.

Another barrier to entry are the district silos. In the past I have said that, "Issues transcend boundaries but voters do not." I would actually change that and add cash so it would be, "Issues and cash transcend boundaries but voters do not." The only way for voters to have impact is to get out of their silo because the decision-making you need may not be in your district. That's why you have to reach out.

Think about it, as an average person trying to reach out to a senator in another state, you won't get through unless you live in that state. One recent improvement has been the development of the Internet, which enables platforms people can use to speak out, build coalitions, and make a difference.

TWO

HOW TO INFLUENCE POLICY
CHANGE LIKE THE TOP 1%

▭

SUSAN: Talk to us about the problems someone needs to overcome to start effectively influencing policy change.

JOHN: There are three problems people face when they try to get something done:

1. Apathy
2. Access
3. Affordability

If you are apathetic and don't engage, you won't get anything done, so you have to get past that first.

Second, you really need to have access to a lawmaker, but you also need to be able to effectively build coalitions of people who believe the same thing you do.

The third problem, which is sometimes missed, is

affordability. You have to have the time or resources to mount a campaign and get something done.

You want to get clear on your message, bring together people who share your point of view, and have sufficient money or resources to mount a campaign to keep the whole effort going. The people on top, people in government affairs, large corporations that have government affairs offices and lobbyists, do that every single day.

SUSAN: Are you suggesting the reader hire a lobbyist?

JOHN: In some ways, yes. Let me explain. We have been jaded by the media, which is always saying lobbyists are bad because they control the game.

Television, media and big newspapers lobby. It's really part of the hypocrisy of democracy where they say, "Do as I say, not as I do." They have had an impact on FEC decisions as well as lobbying committees in the House and Senate but it's really just for them, not the little guys.

So, a simple way of thinking about this is, if you can't beat 'em, join 'em. If you can't beat them, the right answer is not to destroy public property or become an anarchist. That doesn't help anybody. You have to engage in a strategic way.

It's no different than if you had a complex tax problem as an individual, a small business, or a company. You hire tax experts to navigate the world of complex tax issues for you. If you have a problem medically, you hire the best surgeon, or you go to the best hospital you can. If you have a problem with the government, instead of waiting until you have to go to court to solve something, be proactive. Get involved in the legislation beforehand or hire an expert to do it for you.

You don't have to learn everything and do it all yourself. There are experts doing it already, and they have built relationships. We refer to them as public affairs people, lobbyists, or political affairs consultants. Those are the folks you would hire.

When I looked at this as a model of what a successful campaign does I noticed there are three things you need to make all this work: (1) message, (2) mass, and (3) money.

You have to have a clear message or idea about what you want to get done. Often, when groups come together, they shout out epithets and slogans, and they chant, but they're generally just making big assertions of what they want to get done. They'll say, "Justice for all!" or, "No more war!" or, "Save the whales!" In reality, they need to drill down deeper and say, "I support H.R.2095," the Fair Pay Act of 2017 related to equal pay, or whatever their cause is.

Politicians speak in terms of actual bills, so it's important for you to align yourself with a bill, which is in a legislative body. You'll know who's supporting it, what committee it's in, who the sponsors are, and who is already taking it seriously. A lobbyist I spoke to in Washington told me, "I don't care what ideas you have; I can tell you that for every idea you have, there is a bill in Congress reflecting that idea." I thought that was pretty powerful.

The second thing you need is a mass of people. You also need to authenticate the voter or constituent. It's easy for a politician looking out their window at folks protesting in the streets and say, "That's not my constituent out there," but they don't really know because the individual is not identified. If the individual were identified by district in some way or made it clear who they were, it would actually change the equation.

In the past, I've used a simple example: If people were marching on the Washington Mall, wearing distinctive t-shirts that didn't just have the message, "Equal justice," but also said, "California 18," "Wyoming 1," or, "Florida 3," (CA-18), (WY-1), (FL-3), those codes would cause the lawmaker to realize the voters from their district were in the streets, and they would pay more attention. I think the media would also pick up on that and take it much more seriously.

You can't be random about this. You need to make sure your issue is clear, you know who the constituents are, and your cause is aligned with the right committee members debating the bill as it runs through the congressional halls and committees. One of the things we focus on at iLobby is C.I.C.A.S. It stands for Constituent-Issue-Committee-Alignment-Strategy. You need that alignment or roadmap.

And finally, you want to make sure that if you bring in a lobbyist, their practice area and expertise matches the issue you care about and are advocating for.

All of this sounds tremendously complex, but it's the job of the lobbyist to walk you through it, putting some of this complexity in the background, so you don't get over-whelmed.

The third part of this is money. If you don't have money, you cannot sustain a message. If you pay for a bus trip to Washington or a flight or hotel, you've already incurred an expense of several hundred dollars.

Let's take a simple example. If there were a million person march on the Washington mall, do you think that every person there might've spent at least $100? I mean bus fare, transit, hotel, lunch, coffee, sunscreen, a bottle of water? It adds up. How much of that spending went to pushing their issue forward? What they are hoping for is that the media will give them some airtime and they'll end up on television or eventually YouTube. But does that really inform the lawmaker about what they want in a specific way? No. So 1 million people, $100, they could potentially have $100 million at their disposal which would've been way more than almost any other single donor or corporate advocate on an issue related campaign.

SUSAN: Makes sense. What are you suggesting?

JOHN: Well, if you could do this another way and pool your funds with others, you could hire a representative to reach your representative.

In other words, you would do what companies do when they hire lobbyists or trade associations and pay dues: They offset the individual cost by sharing the total cost and allowing more people to come in at a reduced price.

It's just cost sharing, no different than what exists in the sharing economy with Uber or any number of companies. If you share costs, you are then able to afford what had previously been a very expensive resource, and out of the reach of most people.

Lobbying, historically, has been very expensive, $500,000 to $1 million a year, with no guarantee the lobbyist will be successful. On the other hand, you have the ability to influence and get something done at a much lower cost.

There are now a number of public affairs and lobbying firms in Washington and elsewhere who want to represent smaller clients who can't afford the big bucks and do so at a fraction of the cost. As they emerge, more people can take advantage of them.

SUSAN: Why do you think public affairs firms are willing to go with that approach and work with smaller clients, rather than continuing to work with large corporate clients?

JOHN: I think they have realized they want to work directly with smaller clients and give them access to the halls of Washington, the political corridors, but they've also realized there's money being left on the table. There is a lot of waste associated with large companies and big government.

I recently heard a story of a large lobbying firm hiring interns or junior associates and have those people sit in on committee meetings or go to Washington just to take notes. The firms charge clients $200 an hour or more and the intern makes about $25 an hour.

It's pretty valuable for them. But you also realize now we have C-SPAN and so many other media outlets to provide information. They don't need clerks and interns sitting in on committee meetings, taking notes and then providing them to the client. The firms are trying to make themselves look good, but people are realizing there's a more efficient way of doing that.

There is ultimately a cheaper way to do it, but you have to be willing to put some money into the game if you're serious.

. . .

SUSAN: How is this different from just petitioning or attending town hall meetings?

JOHN: In the case of petitions, generally one author writes one and makes it available. You have probably had someone come up to you at the supermarket and ask you to sign their petition. It's one and a half pages of fine print. You don't really know what it's about, and you're not in the position to comment on it with your kids in tow, needing to be at the next soccer game.

Online petitions are similar. One person authors a petition, which is usually very one-sided because the author is petitioning to get something specific done. There's no room for debate. You either agree or disagree with the entire body of the petition. I think it's important for people who have other opinions and take other positions to be able to have input, debate a topic and have some level of control. A petition doesn't do that well.

Also, many of the people you encounter with petitions are hired and paid by companies to collect signatures. As long as you indicate you're a voter in the district and you can sign the petition with a valid signature, the person administering the petition is paid between $2 and $5, sometimes more, per signature. Petitions are often no different than surveys. They're a little bit biased, and people are hired to administer them. They may not reflect true opinions.

An online debate format, on the other hand, is similar in some ways to a town hall meeting. You have the ability to speak up, make your voice heard, and be recorded. You get to engage in debate, you are able to add to the arguments or add some information that could be helpful to a lawmaker in making a decision about a particular upcoming vote. It's basically crowd sourcing but in an actionable way.

This is important because you are trying to sway the politician, and there's nothing wrong with that. If you have an opinion or facts and think you can be helpful to your representative, they want to hear what you have to say. In some cases, they may agree with you and then you don't need to convince them.

If they have the facts wrong, they've been misguided, or they don't have the full picture, then you definitely want to influence them by sharing new information, which may cause them to rethink their vote, and votes, in aggregate, and change policies. And policy drives law. A politician votes on a piece of legislation. If the bill goes through and the next body and the executive sign it, whether it's the president or the governor, that bill becomes law. People wonder why we end up with bad laws. I think it's because not enough people came forward early on to express their ideas about what should be in the laws. Then they are surprised in January by all the new laws they're forced to comply with.

SUSAN: People need to understand they play an important role in the decision making process. They are the 'boots on the ground'. The politician doesn't necessarily know the correct answer to everything. You may be the domain expert.

JOHN: That's absolutely correct. She cannot be an expert on every single thing, although she should be aligned with and interested in her community. You don't want a politician who's a former astronaut on the agriculture committee, for instance.

I have an intern working with me now who was an intern in Congress for a well-known senator. He said people don't realize they can just walk into the halls of Congress. If they can get through security, anybody can walk in. You don't need an appointment. You can knock on a politician's door and say, "I am a constituent in your district, and I would like to get something done," or, "I have an opinion about this." You won't necessarily get an audience with them, but there's nothing preventing you from trying at the state, local, or federal levels.

THREE
FIVE MISTAKES PEOPLE MAKE WHEN TRYING TO INFLUENCE POLICY CHANGE

SUSAN: Talk about some of the mistakes you see people make when they try to influence policy.

JOHN: There are five key mistakes, which happen on a very general level.

- 1) People complain and blame. They complain about what's going on with the politicians. They hate Washington, and they hate the press. They don't think they're running things right, they don't think the right politician got elected, they think people are stupid, etc. They complain about things, but they don't have solutions themselves. Politicians are sometimes guilty of this as well, blaming the other party.
- 2) You talk to the wrong people. You talk to your friends at work or your next-door neighbor

or your dog. You may have really good opinions about what needs to change, but if you never express those opinions to politicians or your lawmakers, then you're talking to the wrong people. There are many reasons you do this. You don't feel you know the topic well enough, you think you could be wrong. Or you're generally insecure about what you think you know about politics because you believe politics are only for the informed, the powerful and the rich.

- 3) Fuzzy thinking. People often have two or three key facts. You listen to fake news, and you end up not really understanding the complexities of an issue. Many things are complicated, but common sense can also be applied to them. You can boil most things down to simple solutions and get clear on the framework of an issue before you get bogged down in the details.

- 4) Focusing on celebrity candidates and not the issue. People were anti-Trump, pro-Hillary, or pro-Bernie-Sanders, particularly during the presidential campaign. They focused on the executive branch and the backgrounds of the candidates, their tax returns, their attitudes, their status, whether or not they talked to the Russians, if they were involved in indiscreet activities in the past. What does all that have to do with putting in a new sidewalk or a new stop sign in your local town or city? What does that have to do with having a consistently clear energy policy or a working healthcare plan that will be decided by Congress?

People like political gossip. They think it makes a difference to talk about it. The people who are serious about policies and issues, however, move through the arguments related to getting things done and don't focus on gossip. They focus on confronting issues and solving problems. They don't follow personality. They focus on policy. They follow the money.

- 5) The fifth mistake is failing to build effective coalitions. You can't effect change alone. You're ONE of 700,000 people in your district. You're one small voice. If you gathered together 20 or 100 friends through your social media networks around a single issue, you could begin to build coalitions. You would not be having general discussions about a politician, but would have more specific discussions about issues; healthcare, the debt, education, cyber security or stop signs or speed bumps in your town to slow down traffic so your kids don't get hurt. When people come together around an issue, have an understanding of it, and communicate it to the right person, they can solve all the problems I just mentioned.

FOUR

THE BIGGEST MYTHS ABOUT
POLITICS AND GOVERNMENT

SUSAN: It can be difficult to get to the facts of any situation, especially one where there is so much hearsay or anecdotal evidence about what is effective. What are some things people believe about government or policy change that just aren't true?

JOHN: People think lobbyists are bad. They neglect to realize lobbyists work for clients. It's no different than when you hire an attorney. He or she or the firm needs to check to make sure they have no conflicts of interest before they help you, and they need to make sure what they're doing for you is clear.

People hear the bad stories about how lobbyists are corrupt and what they do they do poorly, yet the same media outlets that say lobbying is bad use lobbyists themselves to affect legislation. I think the public has been done a disservice by thinking they can effect change all on their own or thinking that voting once every four years is enough. It isn't.

People also think, in some respects, political problems are beyond fixing, but that's a nihilistic approach. To think you have no power and your opinion doesn't matter is a complete myth.

I believe people have dignity, intelligence, foresight, and common sense, and those qualities as human beings allow us to say, "You know what? We have a way of solving problems in our communities. We are, in fact, the boots on the ground in our communities. We understand the problems, so we can arrive at solutions and move issues forward." It becomes a question of confidence and clarity and people realizing they can get things done.

People assume the president has the power to solve all problems. We don't talk about the individual elected members, and instead we talk a lot about the executive branch. The executive branch does not pass laws; the legislative branch does. The president can only write executive orders, which then go to the agencies, which promulgate the rules and regulations that have the force of law. One president's executive orders can all be undone by the next executive in office. To think the executive branch has all the power to get things done is a misunderstanding of how the three bodies of government work together: the judicial, the executive, and the legislative branches.

Many people who lack confidence think they have to be an attorney to do this. That's not true. Individuals, under the First Amendment, have the right to petition the government for redress of grievances. That has been our right for more than 200 years. It's one thing we have in this country, which other countries don't have; certainly not tyrannies.

Freedom of speech, freedom of assembly, and freedom

of the press are rights we need to continue to value. You don't need to be an attorney or even a professional to express your opinion in a civil way.

Another myth is once in office, politicians will do what they promised on the campaign trail. When you analyze a politician, particularly as they campaign and after they are elected, you want to see an alignment between their issues, their accomplishments, and their promises.

If they promise something during a campaign, you want to see something in their background related to that. It's no different than a resume. If they accomplished that in the past, the likelihood is if they promise it, we believe it, and we hope they continue to do it in the future.

After they are elected, we expect them to do the things they said they would. People often believe they will, and then once they get in office, they say, "I couldn't pass that because things changed, and the other party had more power and prevented me from doing it." They don't stand on principle. They back away from some of the promises they made, and they make them seem complicated or like there weren't enough votes. Ultimately, they backtrack from the promises they made to the voter on the campaign trail.

That results in the feeling many people have that politicians are insincere. A recent Gallup poll revealed our trust of Congress is down to about 20%. That lack of trust happens consistently. Trust in Congress has ranged from about 10% to 20%. We don't believe what politicians say or do because they unwind their promises and positions all the time.

I've spoken to a lot of folks who are apathetic and say they don't have any issues. In reality, we all have issues because everything in our lives is so regulated, from minimum wage to whether or not we can have a pool of water in our backyards to EPA regulations to eminent domain, where cities or counties can say they're going to offer you market value for your land so they can put up a telephone line.

You can go blissfully through life and ignore all that, saying it doesn't affect you, but in reality, all these issues affect you all the time.

One of the more subtle things we tend to neglect is that there are laws on the books dating back from 100 years ago which have never been taken off the books, and it's unlikely they will be unless somebody says, "This is a ridiculous law. Let's get rid of it." For example, you could find yourself standing on the beach in Santa Monica wearing shorts and be fined $25 or $50 because of a law from 1920 stating you have to wear a bathing suit down to your ankles. Issues affect all of us, even on the beach.

SUSAN: Why is this so important?

JOHN: Follow the money. Every year we pay taxes; income tax, Social Security, payroll tax, property tax, gas tax, workers comp, bicycle licenses, gun permits, liquor tax, small business surtax. The list goes on and on. So we pay to cover a budget of $3.8 trillion. Now most of that is mandatory spending for Medicare and Social Security. But there's about $1.2 trillion that's discretionary and those are your tax dollars and someone else has figured out how to spend your money.

If you care about getting ahead you need to have a say in how it's spent and what programs the government takes on. It requires more than just voting once every four years. You

need to get into the game. By not playing, it's costing you...
a lot.

It's like giving your teenager $50 every day and you
don't know how he's spending it. It just disappears and he
just keeps asking for more. And you think he's making good
decisions?

President Reagan had this famous quote where he said,
"The government's view of the economy could be summed
up in a few short phrases. If it moves, tax it. If it keeps
moving, regulate it. And if it stops moving, subsidize it."

FIVE

"THERE OUGHT TO BE A LAW"

SUSAN: Can you share some examples of people who have been successful in swaying policy?

JOHN: The most interesting examples I can think of occurred as a result of a politician reaching out to his community and saying, "I want to hear from you." From 2002 to roughly 2012, state Senator Joe Simitian in Silicon Valley, California ran a contest called "There Ought to Be a Law."

During that time, he received several hundred submissions for laws per year. He would select the ones he and his staff thought had the best chance of becoming law and promised to sponsor the bills on the Senate floor. He would corral his colleagues and move forward on the issues. The person who won the contest received a flag that had flown over the state capitol, some press attention, and the opportunity to be there when the bill was read on the Senate floor.

It takes great courage for an individual to come forward and say, "Here's an idea I want to solve in my community." Senator Simitian held this contest for a number of years, and now the senator who took over his position is doing it. A handful of other assemblymen and senators in California are doing it as well, and it's traveled as far as Pennsylvania! Having a lawmaker sponsor something one of his constituents brings forward is a great way to actively engage citizens.

I spoke to Senator Simitian, and he said, "The ideas that came from the public were things that we never would have thought of while we were in office. It just wouldn't have occurred to us."

If you go to www.senatorsimitian.com/oughta, the website for "There Ought to Be a Law," you can find example after example of bills that passed. People were empowered to move forward and get things done. They had the opportunity to speak out.

Another successful example is an 86-year-old gentleman from San Jose who for years pursued getting a bill signed into law. It's taken him a long time but he finally got two bills sponsored and they are in 115th Congress now, H.R. 1706 and H.R. 1707. So in addition we did a podcast with him on his efforts and set up a debate so more people could be aware of his issue related to the Italian American community and their mistreatment in WWII. But to get a sponsored bill in Congress, that was all his own effort and he did a great job of moving that forward. Chet Campanella, it's a great story of persistence and dedication to a cause.

On the other end of the spectrum was a young student. A school in Pennsylvania had the idea for the students to enter There Oughta' Be a Law contest by writing an essay.

A 10-year-old girl, Paige Flinchbaugh, in one of the classes, didn't think students at the school got enough exercise because only 15 minutes a day was allocated to it. The school had less time for physical education.

Paige's proposal for increased exercise time reached Senator Ryan Aument's office. He read it, he liked it, and he sponsored the bill. At 10 years old, Paige had a law changed. You can watch a YouTube video of Representative Ryan Aument interviewing Paige about her law at www. youtube.com/watch?v=MPdzwfZTGOU.

It's pretty touching. If a 10-year-old can do this, you can too.

SUSAN: You mentioned the money earlier. Can you elaborate on that a little?

JOHN: Sure. One of the really interesting initiatives is the movement toward the Participatory Budgeting Project. Some communities in Boston, Chicago and St. Louis are using this to invite the public into how government dollars are spent. Their only concern is that more people are not yet participating, but it's a great movement that is picking up steam. I believe it started in Brazil about 20 years ago and it is now in over 1000 cities around the world and dozens of other communities in the US.

SIX

HOW TO BEGIN TO CHANGE A LAW IN LESS THAN 60-MINUTES

SUSAN: The person reading this book is the one who, more than anyone, knows what needs changing. If they are inspired to make a difference, what is the most effective use of their time, money and energy?

JOHN: There are so many ways in which people try to reach politicians, and so many ways fall short or go awry. As part of my background, I worked in government affairs at a large entertainment company in L.A. in the mid-1990s. I know most people never had that experience. We worked with politicians, attorneys, lobbyists, the public and the administration and we got things done at all levels of government. From this experience I realized that more people needed to understand how this process works. So fast forward a number of years and I started working on this platform. I wanted to share some of the ideas I thought would work to help people engage.

We created an online debate platform called iLobby, where people post issues or "debates" online. They put something they want to get done, a law they want to change or repeal, for instance, at the federal, state, or local level; in very simple, colloquial language.

Other people on the platform can vote on that issue, either, "Yes, I agree" or, "No, I disagree." If they have comments, they can add an argument, or several arguments.

There is a cutoff time for the debate, and once it's reached, we take a look at how many people support the issue, how many don't, their arguments, and the districts those people are from. We aggregate all this information to either be presented to a politician or crowdfunded. If an issue is crowdfunded, we use the money raised for them to hire a lobbying firm to represent the issue and take it even further. So it solves the three problems I mentioned earlier, apathy, access and affordability.

This format allows anybody to bring up an issue and debate it. The difference between this and what Senator Simitian did is that Senator Simitian's idea only applied to his district. With 3,000 counties around the country and 30,000 cities in 50 states, it would take a huge effort for each lawmaker to take on voters' suggestions on top of everything else they're doing. One of the reasons they can't do it is they're generally spending half their time raising money for the next election. Anyway, if they did take it on, it would take a very long time, plus they don't have the staff and they still have the cross-district constraint issue.

We decided to put some issues on the Internet. They are available to anyone in any district. Visitors to our site can find the issues that matter to them, and if they don't, they can create their own issues, share with their friends and co-workers, and begin to build coalitions. This goes back to the idea of getting clear on your message, building a mass of people, and if you're serious, putting your money where your mouth is, so you can move forward in an open, nonpartisan way.

SUSAN: The site sounds like a great way for someone to build momentum and get other people involved, without having to go out and find them. What responsibilities do individuals have to spread the word about their cause and engage people at a local level?

JOHN: You have to advocate for your own idea or position and be willing to put yourself out there, sharing it with your friends or your employees. I think when people have a common problem; they come together and look for a way to solve that problem using the wisdom of the crowd.

Politicians do not have the answers to all the problems. I think that's evident from the kinds of laws and legislation we see come down the pike. Part of the problem is there are warring factions in Congress fighting to get their particular thing done, and the public is left out of the debate. You don't have a seat at the table.

I think it's important for average individuals to be present and to participate in a very simple way. You can engage in a debate on our website on an iPhone, an iPad, or your computer, and it only takes a couple minutes. You don't have to get on a bus, you don't have to spend money to fly to Washington, and you don't have to set up a meeting with a representative. You get to give your input, and it gets aggregated in such a way that it's compounded with the support of more people.

SEVEN

TAKE ACTION

SUSAN: What is the best advice for someone looking to get started?

JOHN: There are a couple ways to start.

You might feel the need to read a fair amount before taking action but it's not necessary. If you'd like, you can read my book, *"How to Change a Law."* There's a chapter on the specific steps you need to take.

It's really very simple. You find an issue and vote on it. If you want to comment, you make an argument. You can start your own debate and share it with your friends. The more you share it, the more people know about it, and over time, you'll find people who support your position. Having people who support your position is critical. They don't have to be just the people in your neighborhood. In the case of an issue at the federal level, you need to remember that the people who are deciding on an issue are in all different states.

If my issue is related to something in California and my Aunt Mary lives in Texas and her representative is the chairman of that committee, it will help me if Aunt Mary votes on my issue since she is the chairman's constituent. That makes all the difference in the world.

If you, a small group, or an advocacy group wants to take an issue to the next level, you have a choice. You can do it yourself (DIY) or find a government affairs firm that will do it for you, do it for me (DFM) for a fee.

This could move your issue forward and do so a little bit faster than you might on your own.

SUSAN: What is your role in all this?

JOHN: I'm passionate about this because I think more people need to be engaged in the political process. I think we currently have a deficit in political literacy in this country.

If you remember, financial literacy became more widespread in the 1970s when the public got into investing. Initially, most people didn't understand mutual funds until Morningstar came along and educated them. Most people didn't understand discount brokerage until Schwab came around, but both of these concepts were available to the very wealthy as far back as the 1920s, '30s, and '40s. They've been around for a long time, but average folks didn't have access to them. But the rich did.

I think political literacy is making the same transition. It's the next big hurdle. People need to learn how politics works, understand how the government works, and cherish what we have, compared to failed states or dictatorships where they have no input and no democracy. It's important for people to get involved.

Democracies exist in the United States, Germany, France, Canada, Australia, New Zealand, and other countries. But there are probably over 100 second and third world nations where people don't have a voice or opportunities to get things done. In those countries, small groups at the top set the agenda and run everything, taking advantage of individuals who could otherwise have better lives. I think people worldwide want to have a say in their affairs, in the life of the nation.

SUSAN: The generation coming up seems to be very active in wanting to influence policy changes. They want to change the country, they want to change the world, and they want to be active participants.

You've built a platform for them to leverage their knowledge and enthusiasm; they just need to engage with it.

JOHN: Pretty much. I see iLobby as an actionable platform, and it stems from my experience in government affairs for a number of years.

I also think for people or business owners who are intellectually curious, policymaking is a lot of fun because it's one big, hi stakes, ever-changing, competitive game.

I know you need to figure out your issue and find people who support, like, and agree with you; however, you must allow them to debate because they could give you ideas contrary to your current point of view, and that's a good thing. If you're serious about the issue, put some money in the pot, and try to raise as much money as you can. Then hand off all that complexity to someone who does the rest for you, who's doing it every day and who has the relationships and knowhow. A former U.S. president recently said, "People need tools, training, networks, relationships and funding to be effective." I agree with that.

At iLobby we simply act as a matchmaker between voters and lobbyists. Lobbyists have access to politicians. You could do this all on your own, but I guarantee you it's complicated. If you are one group, or even a group of five people, and you go see a lawmaker, you have to realize they are also meeting with the ten largest trade groups and the ten largest companies in the world. Your small group of five people isn't going to do much.

If you came in from a platform, however, and have 20,000 voters behind you, every one of whom put in $30, you could say that you'd raised $600,000. If that were true, you could be in the office of any Washington lobbyist tomorrow morning. It's that simple. Skip the movie, save the $30 and shape your destiny.

SUSAN: That access is hugely important. The 1% can buy that access just because of who they are. When the average person connects with 20,000 other like-minded individuals, they become like the 1% with influence. That means politicians will take their phone calls, answer their emails, and sit down with them.

JOHN: Exactly. You basically become a client of the lobbying firm. This is a game. If you enter the game, play by the rules, and don't violate the law, then you're operating within the rules they all understand because you've engaged in civil discourse and because you have real voters aligned with the right lawmakers on the right committees who support your issue.

The support of real voters in real districts is really important. A company could say they have a plant in your community or they can add jobs to your community if you go along with their thinking, but they may not have the voters. The most important thing for politicians is serving their constituents.

This platform is about collaborative communication between a politician and voters, and it works both ways. Politicians can initiate change as well; it doesn't have to be initiated by an individual voter. A politician could say, "I want to get the opinion of my constituents, so I'm going to put something up on the site and see if we can get feedback." It would save them a lot of time.

In fact, we did this at the local level in a town near me with a non-controversial issue. The town was small, and the leaders wanted feedback from residents on an issue. We worked with the city manager and the mayor to draft their debate, and we put it up on the site.

In a very short time, within a matter of days, they got votes, feedback, and data about what people wanted. That helped them make a decision about the issue they wanted to move forward with.

They didn't have to print a letter and send a copy to everybody. People circulated the issue by simply sharing it with their friends' list on Facebook. A greater number of people responded to that debate than would have if they had gone through the normal channels.

Remember Susan, I'm not saying this is a replacement

for your other advocacy efforts. What I am saying is if you are protesting and writing letters to your representative by all means keep it up. This is something in addition, another tool to add to your tool belt that is so radically different and maybe more effective - it's a new way of doing things, a new way of thinking about getting involved in the policy process.

WHEN YOU SIGN UP, you have the ability to author content on the site, and you can vote in debates. Voting is like dipping your toe in the water and saying, "Okay, I'm going to take a position on an issue, even if it's not something that matters to me or is in my district." You're just helping somebody else by putting your toe in the water, casting a vote, and saying, "I'm here." But it could help them because the lawmaker/decision maker could be in your district, only you don't know it. You help them. They help you. It's called as author Robert Cialdini writes in his book "Influence," reciprocal altruism.

A lot of people wonder why they haven't heard of this before. I explained that. It's not well known, yet. This isn't for everybody, and we know that, but it will help you discover if you are completely uninterested in politics, or if you're a little frustrated by the political process and think, "This could help me move my business ahead." It will help you figure out if this is right for you and generate some influence or sway in your community.

SUSAN: My final question. I have to ask you this. Why the conch shell on the cover?

· · ·

JOHN: The conch is a powerful communication symbol borrowed from William Golding's novel, Lord of the Flies. He who holds the conch holds the power of civilization and order and when you see one on the beach all you have to do is pick it up and speak.

EIGHT

HERE'S HOW TO START TO INFLUENCE POLICY RIGHT NOW

YOU PROBABLY ALREADY KNOW THAT you're frustrated by politics and the policies that come out of Washington and the state capitols. What you don't know is how to improve it or solve it.

That's where we come in. We help people find a simpler, better, more efficient way to begin to work with your lawmaker, and your community to begin to get something done.

EXPRESS YOURSELF WHERE YOU CAN. Your simple vote will help others. Participate in debates and lend your voice to causes in your community near and dear to you.

IF YOU ARE FRUSTRATED by politics, but you don't

know or think there's a way to make a difference, now with iLobbyco.com there really is a way.

It doesn't have to be complicated and you don't need to be a political science major. You can find a way to move forward and begin to improve your community, influence the country, and impact the world.

REVIEW

If you liked this book, please fee free to leave an honest review. Just a line or two would be very helpful. I want you to know that I will definitely read your review. Thanks so much. Here are the links.

Sway

US
http://www.amazon.com/review/create-review?&asin=Bo7DLJM22C

Goodreads
https://www.goodreads.com/review/new/40594366-sway

Author's Direct Audio Book
https://shop.authors-direct.com/products/sway-the-inside-secrets-the-top-1-use-to-influence-policy-change-and-get-what-they-want-and-how-you-can-too?_pos=1&_sid=afod2b553&_ss=r

Preview: This book is a do-it-yourself manual for voters, small business owners, lobbyists, and policy advocates who want to take political action, influence leaders and change laws.

Once you understand the power of lobbying, you will be able to improve your community, influence leaders, and impact the world.

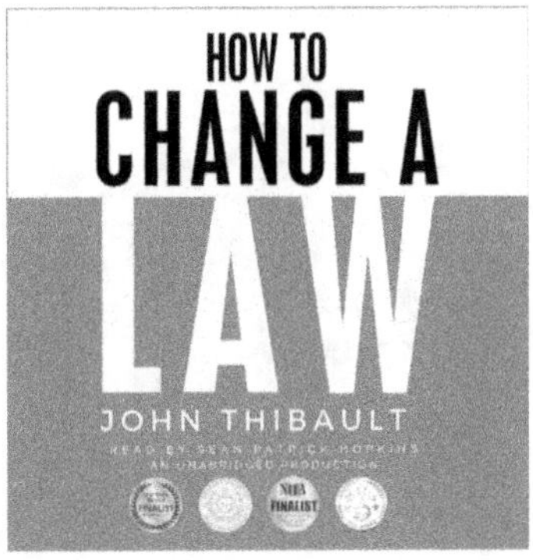

How To Change A Law offers insight, actionable tools, and strategies that will lead you to becoming an active Citizen Legislator who realizes that their participation in public policy matters.

We are at a turning point in our politics; everyone needs to get involved, come together, build coalitions, fund initiatives, and intelligently pursue their agenda.

How to Change a Law

How to Change a Law (Audible)

ABOUT THE AUTHOR

John Thibault is the founder and CEO of Silicon Valley startup, iLobby and the author of the #1 International bestseller "How to Change a Law" and "Sway."

John Thibault is an award winning author and the founder and CEO of Silicon Valley startup, iLobby. He wrote the #1 International bestseller, bestseller "How to Change a Law," "Sway" and "The Political Game."

Previously he served in government affairs at MCA/Universal. He was also the first VP of business development and marketing at eBay and the first VP of marketing at Financial Engines.

He has been published in Association News, Manufacturing Today, CEO for High Growth Ventures and Millennial Magazine, and been interviewed on Amazon TV, and numerous radio affiliates for ABC, CBS, and NBC, podcasts and recently served on a panel for the "Tales of the Cocktail" Foundation.

He holds a Bachelor's degree from Ryerson University and an MFA from UCLA. He is a two-time cancer survivor, enjoys skiing and lives with his wife and three children in Northern California.

"If you've found this book useful, please consider leaving a short review on Amazon."

x.com/ajohnthibault

instagram.com/ilobby.co

amazon.com/author/johnthibault

goodreads.com/John_Thibault

ABOUT ILOBBY

iLobby is an online platform that makes it easy for voters, small business and trade associations to take political action by engaging in public policy.

iLobby connects voters with lobbyists to change laws.
People use iLobby to debate issues, seek resolution to political problems in the world or their community, and to discover, share and express what is important to them.

 facebook.com/ilobby.co

AWARDS

<u>How To Change a Law</u>

- **Gold Medal Winner**, Readers' Favorite Awards, 2017
- **Finalist,** 14th Annual American Book Fest, 2017
- Finalist, 11th Annual National Indie Excellence Book Awards, 2017
- Runner-Up, San Francisco Book Festival, 2017

<u>iLobby</u>

- **Finalist**, Community of Democracies "Annual Democracy Contest," 2016 Warsaw, Poland
- Quarterfinalist, Pepperdine University Most Fundable Companies, 2020, 2021

HOW TO MAKE YOUR VOICE HEARD

Maybe you want to **change a law**? Or maybe you just want to know why every time you write to your Congressperson you get a canned response.

Then you feel like you really don't have a say. There has to be a *better way*.

Find out the 6 things you might be doing wrong and get on the path to finally **making your voice heard**.

SHARE YOUR STORY

If you have a story about how you changed a law, we would love to read it. It could be at the local, state or any level of government. We just ask that it be true, personal, and please keep it under 1200 words.

If your story is accepted, we may include it in a future version. Readers find these stories empowering, and it helps them believe that they can make a difference.